NIRVANA
NEVERMIND

TEXT BY SUSAN WILSON
© UFO MUSIC BOOKS LTD

PHOTOGRAPHS

FRONT COVER © REX FEATURES: KIRK WEDDLE
BACK COVER © RETNA: STEPHEN SWEET

© ALL ACTION
(pages 58, 64, 65)

© PICTORIAL PRESS
(pages 48-50, 65)

© REDFERNS
(page 69)

© RETNA PICTURES LTD
(pages 3, 4, 9, 10, 13-16, 18-20, 22, 23, 25, 26, 28-30, 32-34, 36, 38, 45-50, 52, 54, 56, 62, 63, 68, 71-73, 75, 77, 80)

© REX FEATURES
(pages 6, 7, 40-43, 51, 55, 58-61, 70, 76)

THIS EDITION PUBLISHED IN 1995 BY
UFO MUSIC BOOKS LTD, LONDON, ENGLAND.

PRINTED AND BOUND
BY BUTLER & TANNER LTD
FROME AND LONDON

NIRVANA
NEVERMIND

Susan Wilson

INTRODUCTION

Way up in the North West of America sits a tiny little town full of deserted industrial buildings, characterless precincts and eerily quiet streets. Huge trucks carrying timber rumble through the district, transporting the main trade from the local sawmill's. Fog rolls down from the hills where the rich folks live, clouding the air of the poorer people who dwell in the flats down below. And over on the West side flows the Chehalis River, rushing through this end of America into the Pacific Ocean. Not much happens here in Aberdeen apart from the usual small town drama. By all accounts it's a redneck one-horse place, rife with domestic violence, stoners and suicides. Its history would have probably remained wholly unremarkable in the grand scheme of things had it not been for the legacy of one of its inhabitants. For he was to change the course of its history for all time. His name? Kurt Donald Cobain.

ONE

LOVE BUZZ

At the age of six months, Kurt Cobain moved into the grainy haze of Aberdeen with his mother Wendy and her auto-mechanic husband, Don. Born in nearby Hoquiam on February 20th, 1967, Kurt spent his first few years in Aberdeen as a bright, happy child with an artistic nature. His mother doted on him, recognising his gift for perception early on in his life, and her musical family encouraged Kurt's own musical interest which first expressed itself when he was merely two.

Wendy had a brother, Chuck, who played in a rock'n'roll band, and a sister, Mary, who played guitar. Don and Wendy bought Kurt a Mickey Mouse drum set and Mary introduced Kurt to The Beatles and The Monkees and gave him his first guitar lessons. Unfortunately, she didn't get very far. Her nephew was a hyperactive child who couldn't sit still, and was prescribed the counteractive amphetamine, Ritalin, to keep him calm, before his food allergies were diagnosed. Once his diet had been examined, he was told to avoid sugar and certain additives, and although he quietened down a little as a result, his spirits still soared.

His happy days were numbered though. Kurt's parents were ill-matched, and when their son was eight, they parted, breaking up their home and with it, the sunny kid's heart. He was never quite the same again. From then on he retreated into a world of his own. For a year Kurt lived with his mother, but he didn't like her new boyfriend so she sent him off to Montesano where his father was living in a trailer park. To begin with things worked out. But soon Don announced that he was remarrying and along with his father, new stepmother and two step-siblings, Kurt found himself in a house, with a ready-made family he simply couldn't tolerate. He felt isolated, left out and alone. He fell in with a stoner crowd which prompted his mother to ask his Uncle Chuck to look after him.

The first Nirvana incarnation. From left to right: Chad Channing (_drums_), Chris Novoselic (_bass_), Kurt (or Kurdt as he was calling himself at this time) Cobain (_guitar/vocals_) .

This to-ing and fro-ing characterised Kurt Cobain's early adolescence. He was bumped and bustled around between three sets of aunts and uncles, his paternal grandparents and his immediate family like a ball off a bat. Eventually, when he was 17, he persuaded his mother, who by now was also remarried, to take him back, but it was too late for his sense of security and self esteem to be restored and he never settled with any one member of his family for long ever again.

During this traumatic period of upheaval, Kurt had begun to discover punk rock in a big way. Hanging out with the stoner crowd in Montesano, had introduced him to seventies rock bands like Aerosmith and Black Sabbath, but later he was to read about the Sex Pistols in Creem magazine, a band who completely captured his imagination, even though he'd never heard their records. He began to play guitar and while attending Montesano High School, he met Matt Lukin and Buzz Osbourne, both musicians with a local band called The Melvins. Already partway established on the just-happening Seattle music scene, The Melvins had also contributed to the Deep Six compilation, an album which featured other Seattle prototypes such as Soundgarden, Malfunkshun and Green River. Kurt began roadieing for the band and even auditioned for them once. But most importantly his musical

education was underway, courtesy of Osbourne, who turned him onto all kinds of American underground bands from Black Flag to Flipper.

After he moved back to Aberdeen to live with his mother, Kurt lost touch with his Melvins connections until he met up with Dale Crover, a music fan who frequented the local stoner scene who ended up drumming for the band. At this time, Kurt also noticed Chris Novoselic at High School. Novoselic, an acquaintance of Crover's and a giant of a man, with a totally warped nonsensical humour, appealed to Kurt's sense of otherness, although the two didn't actually begin hanging out together until later, much to Kurt's regret. Bitten by punk, but lonely, Kurt had just two friends in Aberdeen, Jesse Reed and Myer Loftin, although he eventually had to stop seeing Loftin because he was gay, and Kurt was getting too much hassle off the local rednecks to make the friendship possible.

On the homefront, things were beginning to deteriorate again. Kurt had begun to smoke pot heavily, and once more found himself being bandied around between pillar and post. Back to his dad's in Montesano, off with Jesse Reed's Born again Christian parents, and then home once more, he caved in, left school just before graduation, despite the offer of two art scholarships, and got himself a brief spell of employment as a janitor. He lived in

The second Nirvana line up with new recruit Jason Everman (pictured here sat next to Kurt), who was introduced to add more energy to their live performances.

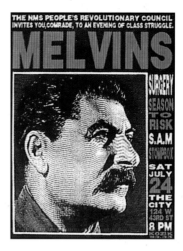

various apartments, on people's floors and doorsteps, and even beneath the North Aberdeen Bridge. After his janitor duties, Kurt worked in a dental surgery, as a swimming instructor and as a hotel cleaner, where he did little more than snatch naps in the empty rooms. The only constant in his life was music.

One of the first bands Kurt ever initiated was Fecal Matter, with Dale Crover on drums and Greg Hokanson on bass. They supported The Melvins and laid down a demo which included *'Downer'*, an instrumental which would reappear on Nirvana's first album, *'Bleach'*. Around this time Kurt got arrested for graffiiting *'Homo Sex Rules'* on the wall of a bank, and he also began to experiment with heroin. Contrary to popular opinion, which paints Courtney Love as the murderous individual who cajoled her husband into smack addiction, Kurt had long been looking for kicks, and his experience of opiates had always been enjoyable. He was impressed with the usual rock'n'roll mythology of heroin and always knew he would at least try it. In a dozy, nowhere town like Aberdeen, where the rainfall is as hard as the residents, drugs are one of the few ways out for kids with hungry minds. Kurt was no exception. He got his first heroin hit around 1986, a good few years before he even laid eyes on Courtney.

Increasingly fed up and disillusioned with the stultifying scene in Aberdeen, Kurt began travelling

to Olympia, home of the alternative Evergreen College (where Sub Pop co director Bruce Pavitt studied punk rock and the ultra hip, ultra independent record label, 'K'. Run by Calvin Johnson and Candace Peterson also of the band, Beat Happening, K would later go on to help spark off Riot Grrl activity, but at this stage was the lynchpin of a small, politically correct, artistic community. Kurt wasn't puritanical enough to soak up the K ethos in its entirety, but he understood the basic message and found it to be a refreshing change from the dead-meat view of Aberdeen. Tracy Marander, his first long-term girlfriend came from Olympia, and eventually Kurt moved in with her, finding solace of a sort within a community more suited to his artistic temperament than his hometown.

Meanwhile, the seeds of Nirvana were being sown. Kurt had begun to play with the loping Chris Novoselic, who shared his love of punk and underground music, as well as the staple seventies rock diet of Aerosmith, AC/DC and Black Sabbath. The pair started out as a Creedence Clearwater Revival cover band called The Sellouts, before hooking up with drummer Aaron Burckhard in what was to be known as 'Skid Row'.

Burckhard was competent enough, although not on the same psychological plain as Chris and Kurt, and after six months or so, he was replaced with Dale Crover, who was on loan from The Melvins. They recorded their first demo under yet another name, Ted Ed Fred, with none other than Jack Endino in the engineering room. Endino, producer of Deep Six, was already establishing himself as a key figure in the Seattle scene, and proved to be instrumental to Nirvana's career when he handed the demo tape to Johnathan Poneman, co-director with Bruce Pavitt of Seattle's up and coming record label, Sub Pop. Poneman loved it, Pavitt wasn't sure, but nevertheless, after a precarious meeting in a Seattle coffee shop, where Chris was drunk and obnoxious and Poneman was his usual businesslike self, the band ended up recording a single for the Sub Pop label.

'*Love Buzz*', a cover tune, originally recorded by Dutch band, Shocking Blue, was released in 1988. Backed with '*Big Cheese*', the single was limited to 1,000 pressings. It now changes hands for anything up to £120. Skid Row were now known as Nirvana, and had recruited Chad Channing on drums. A tiny hippie from Bainbridge Island, who once claimed to have moved house over one hundred times, Chad was first spotted by Kurt and Chris playing with his band Tick-Dolly-Row (alongside Ben Shepherd, now Soundgarden's bassist). His huge North drums attracted their attention and after the trio had bonded through several jamming sessions, it was understood that Chad was in. Everything was finally in place, for the time being at least. Nirvana were ready to roll.

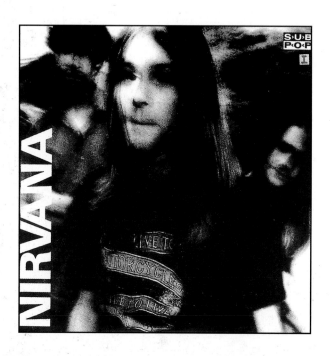

"we feel we can appeal
to more than just the
metal or alternative
markets. we want to
try to be mainstream
too. we want to reach
the Top 40."

KURT COBAIN

IN BLOOM TWO

Once their line-up was set, and once they had a single out, Nirvana decided to get an album ready. Sub Pop had absolutely no money, and usually enabled their bands to record EPs only, but Nirvana had made up their minds, and eventually Pavitt and Poneman coughed up a nominal sum, although the bulk of the finance came from the band's latest recruit - Jason Everman.

Hired by Kurt who wanted to pad out the band's sound, Jason, had known Chad at school and shared a similar background to the trio, although his sullen temperament kept him from ever fitting in completely. On stage he swung his long curls like a metal dude, which embarrassed Chris and Kurt and during tours he retreated to his own little world, barely communicating with the rest of the band. Things were bearable for a while, but it wasn't long before Nirvana felt distinctly uncomfortable with this silent, slightly arrogant addition, whose musical tastes were much too orthodox for them.

Before Jason was actually disposed of though, Nirvana had work to do. They spent December of 1988 in the studio with Jack Endino and managed to eke an entire long player out for $606.17. Dale Crover played drums on *Paper Cuts* and *Floyd The Barber*' while Jason didn't actually play on the record at all, he merely coughed up the budget

money, bumping up the sound in live situations only. But he was given a credit on the album simply because Kurt was feeling charitable. Jason had nothing to do with the songwriting process either.

In fact the songwriting process was a fairly haphazard business. The tunes were there, but the lyrics were literally scribbled down by Kurt at the very last minute, which leaves subsequent analyses of them looking over ambitious and faintly redundant, although the songs were far from nonsensical. Kurt's lyrical outings always consisted of wry, shrewd witticisms, subverted thought patterns and intelligent jokes, and while he consistently denied the presence of any deep personal meaning, subconscious revelations spilt out from time to time.

Nirvana's debut dealt with white trash culture, the local cliques of self righteous Olympia and self conscious Seattle, and general small town scenarios. None of the lyrics were particularly ambitious, they were simply the thoughts and observations of someone from a tiny district who had his own views on his environment. And while Kurt refused to elaborate on them at great length when Nirvana's debut appeared, he more or less stuck with the same lyrical themes, exploring them in more depth on subsequent recordings.

Finally the cover art needed to be completed. After a little bit of deliberation, a Charles Peterson

live shot was agreed on to introduce the world to Nirvana. It was appropriate enough. Peterson was responsible for the look of Sub Pop. His grainy, blurry live black and whites typified the wreckless, amateurish, chaotic genius of the burgeoning Sub Pop/Seattle scene. He pictured local bands throwing themselves around minute venues, swamped by sweaty fans all dressed in what was later to be turned into the *'grunge fashion'* by the world's media. He captured the excitement, the buzz, the original flavour of this new rock community, and his images are still the definitive ones of the period. By June 1989, everything was in place for the release of *'Bleach'*, Nirvana's debut album. Its thick, heavy sound carried echoes of Black Sabbath, whom Kurt and Chris loved, but its ear-grabbing melodies also belied Kurt's punk/pop sensibility. It was a classic

grunge recording, up there with Mudhoney's *'Touch Me I'm Sick'* and Soundgarden's *'Screaming Life'* EPs. It helped to characterise a new sound, a new hybrid of rock- pure seventies' breeze metal, put through the punk blender and mashed into something dirty, murky and wholly unsavoury.

Sub Pop had an eye for this new breed. They understood that it was blossoming on their own doorstep, and they wanted to cultivate and train it. Away from the big corporate business bods of New York and Los Angeles - both longtime American music industry centres - Sub Pop had the chance to re-energise a community and keep it rooted in its geographical origins. like Chicago's Touch And Go, Olympia's K, and Washington DC's Dischord, Sub Pop had the opportunity to bring music back to the people. And despite later attempts at wheelings and dealings and confessions of semi-mock-contrivance, Poneman and Pavitt did just that. They may have locked naive bands into difficult deals (partly because they had a no-contract policy, which Nirvana luckily managed to avoid) but they were responsible for drawing the world's ears to a soggy little part of America, where rainfall is more common than sunshine, where the air is fresh, where coffee is compulsory and where rock music was being re-worked. Despite efforts to reduce the whole happening to a handful of music industry buzzwords, they gave a solid identity to Seattle and its offspring, grunge, initiating a wave of popular cultural activity, the like of which hadn't been witnessed since punk.

Of course the bands were the main staple in all this. Most of them knew each other, having worked together in their small creative network. Trace any Seattle band's family tree and it soon becomes apparent that everyone knows everyone else. But local industry figures, such as Pavitt and Poneman, Charles Peterson, Susan Silver (who promoted rock shows with Pavitt and went on to manage Soundgarden and Alice In Chains) and Jack Endino were instrumental in channelling the artistry. Nirvana, despite their reservations about being manhandled by scene-sculptors, were no exception.

Ever the individualist, Kurt had a sort of capitalist-anarchist attitude from the beginning. He may not have altogether approved of the potentially generic Seattle sound, (although most of the bands were highly distinctive, plenty of bandwagon-hoppers leapt on board during the early nineties but he realised he had to reach people before he could really hit them with a vision. Sub Pop seemed like a perfect way to start.

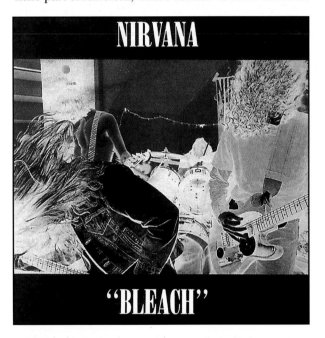

Small enough to retain a personal touch (albeit a somewhat cunning one) and up-and-coming and-hip enough to lend a cool helping hand, the label provided Nirvana with an ideal chance to get a product out to the marketplace.

Products need promotion though, so just after the release of *'Bleach'*, Nirvana embarked on their first tour of America. They headed off in a tiny van to play a total of twenty six shows around the country, on what was to prove a demanding expedition. Tensions were aggravated by the presence of Jason, who was becoming more and more tiresome with his big rock attitude and introverted moods. Chris began to drink even more seriously than he had at home, and eventually the band started trashing their gear at gigs. It was a way of releasing the pent-up stuff which goes with touring, as well as being a kind of jokey, brash rock statement. Finally Jason got to be too much. Nirvana cut their tour short by about a week and drove home in silence after a showcase in New York with fellow Sub Pop band The Fluid. Jason was out. Two weeks later he joined Soundgarden as bass player, but his temperament caused exactly the same problems and after several months he was sacked to make way for Ben Shepherd, Chad's former bandmate. After a stint working for a record company in New York, and then playing with Mindfunk, Jason eventually joined the US Navy in 1994.

After such an unpleasant experience, Nirvana stuck to being a trio. They completed another two week tour, recorded the **'Blew'** EP, and set off for Europe with Tad, another Sub Pop band based just outside Seattle. The overseas trip was gruelling. Both bands shared a bus, and together with Tad Doyle's stomach upsets and various members of his band's porn habits, Nirvana certainly felt the pressure. In Rome Kurt cracked. He threatened to jump off a speaker stack and smashed up a couple of microphones before declaring that he was going home and bursting into tears. Johnathan Poneman was present and calmed him down, but it was pretty obvious that Kurt was suffering from stress. The very early signs of his trouble began to show when

he told Poneman that he didn't respect his audience and that he hadn't formed a band to fulfil these people's demands.

Somehow Nirvana wound up the tour, which culminated with the Lamefest in London, where they trashed four guitars in half an an hour. They returned home in one piece - just about and when they got back, Chris married his long term girlfriend, Shelli. After a short break the band set off on a couple more small tours, and the pressures continued to mount. In May Chris shaved his head after a particularly disastrous show in New York, and Kurt told Sounds music paper that he wanted to kill his colleagues, and that he was thinking of jacking in the whole thing. America was full of retards, he moaned, so what was the point? About to leave the tiny Olympian apartment he'd shared with Tracy, plus six terrapins, three rabbits and a parrot, he was evidently feeling increasingly disillusioned about his career, if not his whole life.

Things weren't helped by Sub Pop's apparent lack of commitment to their artists. Although Poneman had believed in Nirvana right from the start, his label didn't have the financial resources to give them what they really needed and after a couple of months, sales of *'Bleach'* were beginning to be adversely affected by the usual independent label setbacks - poor distribution and limited publicity. Although it did sell, and steadily, Sub Pop had taken their fingers off the button, leaving Kurt frustrated by requests for his record from kids at gigs, who hadn't been able to find a copy.

Fed up with the way things weren't developing, Nirvana decided to take a course of action which was to greatly affect the course of their future career. They decided to look for another label. To compound matters, Sub Pop were actually in trouble. A couple of distribution deals, including one with Columbia, hadn't worked out, and they were cutting back on their roster. Kurt knew his band would be quashed on a business level if they didn't bail out, so with a lot of difficulty (being someone who never enjoyed confrontation) he and Chris broke the news to

Poneman and Pavitt over the course of a few days. They had already laid down the basis of their next album, understood, up until now, to be their second for Sub Pop, so they had a ready-made demo with which to do the record company rounds. And once they'd buried their guilt, they focused themselves on finding a new deal.

Kurt and Chris had one last matter to sort out before they could really pull ahead though. For a while they'd been less than happy with Chad's playing, and at the end of their shows in May, they travelled to his home in Bainbridge Island to break the news to him. Chad, who'd been hoping for greater participation on the songwriting side of things, wasn't too upset at the news, being the philosophical, hippie creature that he is, although there was undoubtedly an element of regret. Questioned later about their former drummer's welfare, Chris remarked that he was quite happy, baking clay fishes back home! Whatever he was doing, Chad continued to drum, and news of his subsequent bands has popped up every now and then.

So - the hunt was on for a new record deal and a new drummer. Before they found either, they recorded one last single for Sub Pop. *'Sliver'* was released in 1990, and featured Mudhoney's Dan Peters on drums. Mudhoney were on hold while their guitarist, Steve Turner, was considering returning to college to study one of the social sciences, so Peters was relatively free of commitments when he stood in for Nirvana. He ended up becoming a semi-permanent member, although only for a few months. Kurt and Chris both loved Mudhoney and wanted no part in encouraging them to split, so when Turner chose rock'n'roll tomfoolery over a serious life of academia, they willingly let Dan go, despite having really enjoyed their term with him.

In the latter half of 1990, Chris and Kurt were in San Francisco rehearsing with their old cohort, Dale Crover for a forthcoming tour supporting Sonic Youth. One night they went to see a Washington DC punk band called Scream, on the Melvins' recommendation, and were completely blown away by the drummer. The timing was perfect. A short while later, Scream's bassist simply vanished in Hollywood, so Kurt's old friend, the good angel Buzz Osbourne, acted as middle-man and arranged for Scream's drummer, Dave Grohl, to fly up to Seattle for a meeting with Nirvana. Dave had already seen Nirvana, at their one and only gig with Dan, and he wasn't overly impressed, although he was intrigued by the personalities involved.

Nirvana wanted Dave Grohl immediately. He was perfect for them. Musically they weren't what Dave was used to, but he wanted in as well.

"The music that Scream wrote was a lot more complex. The beauty of some of Nirvana's pop songs is that they're just so simple. Sometimes less is more."

he said a year after joining.

And so the year that was to transform the lives of Kurt Cobain, Chris Novoselic and new boy Dave Grohl was just about to begin. 1991 saw the fruition of all their labour's. But in many ways, it was also the beginning of their end.

Now with new recruit Dave Grohl (commandeered from the band *Scream*) the final incarnation of Nirvana had been born.

"the beauty of some of nirvana's pop songs is that they're just so simple, sometimes less is more."

DAVE GROHL

THREE
TEEN SPIRIT

When Dave Grohl joined Nirvana, the tape which they had intended to release through Sub Pop was flying around the record industry like a piece of burning gold. Susan Silver had introduced the band to top lawyer, Alan Mintz, Sonic Youth went on to introduce them to their management company Gold Mountain (run by John Silva and Led Zeppelin's ex press officer, Danny Goldberg) and all they had to do was pick a label. Anything Sonic Youth said was cool, was very cool by Nirvana. And it was ultimately Kim Gordon's persuasion which sealed the band's liaison with Geffen Records. One of the main difficulties for any prospective label was buying Nirvana out of Sub Pop, but for a company with big bucks, who intended to treat Nirvana as a serious investment, this didn't really pose too much of a problem. Gary Gersh, the man responsible for signing Sonic Youth, decided that Nirvana were worth the money needed to secure them away from Sub Pop, and by April 31st, 1991, the deal was finalised, inked and official.

Meanwhile, Kurt's private life had been in turmoil. After he split with Tracy Marander, he started seeing Tobi Vail, an Olympian who painted and played with the Riot Grrl band Bikini Kill, but not for long. Kurt wanted more from a relationship than Tobi could give him, and his break-up with her was painful, leaving him feeling lonely for something more permanent. He'd also started experimenting with heroin again, which worried Dave and Chris. The band had a lot of work ahead of them, and besides, they didn't want their friend to be delving into such a dangerous game.

Soon after they finalised their Geffen deal, Nirvana drove down to Los Angeles to begin recording their new material. And this is when Courtney Love entered their lives. The woman who was to put an end to Kurt's loneliness - at least as much as any human being could - was living just a few blocks away from where the band were to stay, and she quickly made her presence felt.

Two years earlier Courtney had met Kurt when she saw Nirvana play a show up in Portland. The pair had felt an instant mutual attraction, and got in touch again through Dave's ex-girlfriend, Jennifer Finch of L7, also a friend of Courtney's.

Courtney Love had already acquired something of a reputation on the alternative rock scene around the world. The daughter of an analyst and one of the Grateful Dead's entourage, she'd lived in New Zealand and Australia as a child, before her mother sent her back to Eugene in Oregon to live with an analyst friend. There, Courtney managed to get herself arrested for shoplifting a Kiss T shirt, and officially became a juvenile delinquent when she

was sent to reform school. As a teenager she discovered stripping was an excellent way of earning money - it enabled her to work flexible hours and pay the rent - so she did it all across America and in Japan. When she was sixteen she travelled to Ireland and England with her friend Robin, and ended up living in Liverpool with Julian Cope for a while.

Back in Portland she met up with Kat Bjelland, also a stripper, and the two started playing in bands together before travelling to San Francisco on Courtney's trust fund where they started up Sugar Baby Doll with Jennifer Finch. Eventually Kat split, moving up to Minneapolis, where she formed Babes In Toyland. Courtney sang with the band for a while but Kat kicked her out, starting a bitter rivalry which

blazed for years. Courtney ended up singing with Faith No More, acting in Alex Cox's movies *'Straight To Hell'* and *'Sid And Nancy'*, and eventually decided to settle in Los Angeles where she set about putting Hole together in 1990.

When Kurt met up with Courtney in LA, it was pretty clear that something was going on between the two of them. But he wasn't ready to launch himself into another relationship. He wanted to hang back and focus on the new record. Showing peculiar strength of mind, he deliberately stayed away from Courtney, determined not to get caught up with someone else just yet. It was probably a wise decision, and anyway he didn't have long to wait. A short while after the release of *'Nevermind'*, Kurt ran into Courtney in

'Nevermind' was released on Geffen in September 1991 and before the end of the year Nirvana would be a household name becoming the music of a generation synonymous with the 'Grunge' scene.

England, where she was accompanying her boyfriend, Billy Corgan of Smashing Pumpkins, and the two had a heated exchange at a London nightclub. About a month later, they finally got together after a Nirvana show in Chicago.

Before Kurt sorted out his love life, the album had to be laid down. The sessions in LA were intense and exciting. Equipment got smashed, Chris got drunk and arrested and Kurt got stoned on cough medicine. Butch Vig was at the production controls. He'd already recorded the tape which had sparked off so much interest for them in the label wars, and his reputation as a worthy underground producer was rock solid. But the mixes turned out too flat, and Andy Wallace was called in to put some edge back. The end result was *'Nevermind'*, a sparkling rock album full of brilliant, impossibly catchy pop songs - an album which would change the world.

Kurt was fully aware of *'Nevermind's'* potential. Ever since Nirvana's days with Sub Pop he'd been hatching plans to hit the public with something they weren't expecting, and while he'd restrained himself for *'Bleach'*, preferring at that stage to introduce himself and his band through the whole Sub Pop/Seattle/grunge explosion, by the time Geffen caught up with him he was ready to let go. Or at least begin to. He knew *'Nevermind'* was palatable. He also knew that in itself it would upset a large contingent of his rock audience,

but being such a perverse creature, that's exactly what he intended. Neither was he adverse to the idea of getting radio play. His inner conflict between success and acceptance and an almost esoteric kind of artistic integrity never resolved itself, but in 1991, Kurt believed he had the strength to see it through. He was excited and wired. He seemed much happier than when Nirvana were still with Sub Pop.

"We feel that we're diverse enough to infiltrate into more than one market," he said, prior to *'Nevermind's'* release.

"We feel we can appeal to more than just the metal or alternative markets. We want to try to be mainstream too. We want to reach the Top 40. Even if the whole of the next album can't get across to that type of audience, there's at least a hit single or two in there."

'Nevermind' was released in September 1991 and sold out within days. In America the initial press run was 40,000, in Britain, 8,000. The albums instant popularity owed more to word of mouth and Nirvana's blistering shows than an industry push. Although Geffen's marketing strategies kicked in later, to begin with they simply weren't needed. Sales were astronomical, and mounting all the time, and by the time Geffen actually did step in, things were going through the roof. In the end, Nirvana managed to outsell Michael Jackson, U2 and Guns'n'Roses.

The interest in Nirvana lay at grass roots level, having been built up steadily through their constant touring, the buzz reverberating around Sub Pop and Seattle (proving the power of localised independent labels) and the excitement generated by their outstanding songs. The summer before *'Nevermind's'* release, Nirvana had sealed their live reputation on tours with Dinosaur Jr, Sonic Youth and at Reading Festival, in the UK and although the pressure was on and their behaviour was more out of control than ever before (with everyone out of it and trashing stuff and generally freaking out left, right and centre), the band had paved the way for their next album.

'*Teen Spirit*', the first single to be taken from '*Nevermind*' compounded Nirvana's success after it began receiving constant MTV airplay thanks to a junior programmer who demanded it be given due attention. Kurt's ambition of making it on the mainstream was being realised. The song became an anthem for an entire generation, who up until now, had no facet of popular culture to call their own. Nirvana gave kids something they could relate to. Their authenticity and anti-image stance was a welcome change in the face of stylised LA rock and the glossy pop machines. Working class boys from broken homes wearing second hand flannel shirts and baggy old cardigans spoke volumes to kids who'd grown up in a failing economy with divorced parents and few prospects ahead of them. Unfortunately. though Kurt wasn't quite as enthusiastic about his role model situation as he might have been. Having simply wanted to make a living from music, he quickly found himself in the bizarre position of spokesperson for the teen and twentysomethings of the Western world. And he soon realised he didn't like it. At all.

Part of the problem for Kurt was the swelling fanbase Nirvana were attracting. the kind of meatheads who'd rejected him in Aberdeen were now frequenting his shows and the band began to grow more and more uneasy about it. Being popular meant being accessible, which laid Nirvana open to all kinds of interpretation by all kinds of folk. And Kurt, who'd expressed distress at the audiences who were showing up to gigs at a much earlier stage in Nirvana's career, was horrified by what he'd created. Courtney no doubt tried to alleviate some of Kurt's guilt. She had always been hugely ambitious, fully believing in the right to success and the power to infiltrate from within. She shared Kurt's capitalist anarchist views, but took them much further and had the desire to really follow it all through. She truly wanted stardom, and found it difficult to accept that her partner felt so tormented by it. It was to be a bone of contention between them for some time, partly because Courtney wanted success so badly and found herself being overshadowed by someone who didn't enjoy it in the slightest.

'Smells Like Teen Spirit' was released by Geffen in November 1991 taken from the album 'Nevermind' with 'Drain You' on the B-side, although the 12" had the tracks 'Even In His Youth' and 'Aneurysm'.

ALL APOLOGIES

FOUR

At the end of 1991, Courtney and Kurt began living together and doing heroin on a regular basis. Over a month later it was pretty clear that the pair were addicted, and before long Kurt's habit was costing him one hundred dollars a day.

Chris and Dave didn't notice at first, but Kurt and Courtney's withdrawal into their own little life quickly became apparent. They more or less shut themselves off from the world, and the fact that 'Nevermind' was now number one all across it. It was almost as if they didn't want to deal with the pressures of fame and success at all, choosing instead to immerse themselves in each other and the warm blur of opium.

Kurt maintained that he took heroin for the excruciating stomach pains which had dogged him for years. No doctor had been able to diagnose his condition, so eventually his only option was to kill the pain if he couldn't be cured. Heroin, with its numbing effect certainly did that. It also made him and Courtney oblivious to what was going on around them, reducing, as it does, all sensation and all feeling into a dull pool of nothing but a false sense of comfort.

Naturally, Courtney was blamed for the couple's addiction. Her loud mouth and attention seeking behaviour made her the perfect target for any contempt, but in fact it was Kurt who initiated the drugtaking. Courtney was simply brave enough to actually go and score.

In January of 1992, Courtney discovered she was pregnant. Kurt wanted her to have a termination because of the damage heroin might have done to the baby, but after going through extensive foetal tests, Courtney decided to keep the child. According to her physician, heroin was only threatening to a baby during the first trimester of pregnancy, so the child was probably in the clear as long as Courtney stopped using immediately.

The reality of a baby made Kurt and Courtney face up to certain facts. If they were going to be parents they had to regain some kind of control over their lives. They both went into detox, but when Kurt set off on tour at the end of the month, his stomach pain returned and eventually he was prescribed methadone in Australia.

When Nirvana hit Hawaii on the course of their tour, Courtney and Kurt got married on February 24th. Courtney wore an antique gown which had belonged to the actress Frances Farmer, Kurt wore pajamas, and Chris and Shelli were not present, because of a bust-up between Courtney and Shelli. Courtney sensed Shelli's disapproval of her drug habits, especially as she was now pregnant, and declared that she didn't want anyone at the wedding who wasn't supportive of her and Kurt's union. Shelli was deeply upset, but later the two women managed to talk it all through and reached an understanding.

Nevertheless, the couple were becoming increasingly separate from Nirvana. Kurt was distancing himself more and more from Gold Mountain and Chris and Dave, wrapping himself up in his newfound world of smack and love. In March, he aggravated the situation further when he decided he wanted a bigger cut of the publishing royalties than his colleagues, from *'Nevermind'* onwards. Naturally Dave and Chris were infuriated, believing Kurt was exhibiting unnecessary amounts of greed, but the songwriter got his way, even though he nearly split the band up in the process.

Kurt's habit had by this stage worked its way up to a four hundred dollar a day deal. He was staring death in the eye and his only option was to detox again. He checked into Cedars-Sinai in August and got out in time for the birth of his and Courtney's baby, Frances Bean. Shortly afterwards, the infamous *'Vanity Fair'*

profile of Courtney appeared.

Courtney willingly gave an interview to Vanity Fair journalist, Lynn Hirschberg, hoping to try and bring attention to herself and Hole. Ever ambitious, she took a very bad turn in this case, and ended up paying for it sorely. Hirschberg relentlessly portrayed Courtney and Kurt as low-life druggies with no ethics, morals or standards. Her depiction of Courtney as a henpecking madwoman, hellbent on clawing her way to the top, was particularly unflattering and Courtney's unfortunate remarks on her drug use resulted in her baby being taken away from her and sent to live with her sister, Jamie for a while. Lawsuits flew around the place, as Courtney tried to prove that a nurse from Cedars-Sinai (where Frances was born) had leaked her medical records to the press, and suddenly the world was pointing its finger at the Cobains. From wild-child post-punk idols, they had switched into evil junkie scum. The entire experience nearly broke them altogether.

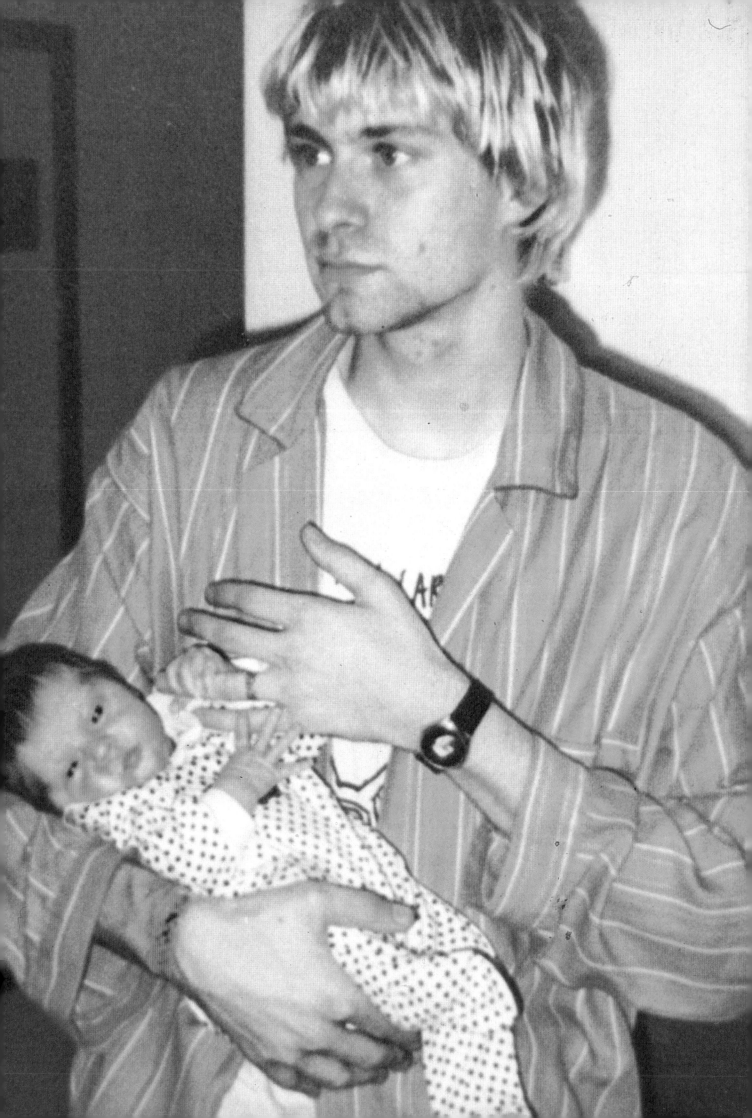

Thereafter the press were a lot tougher on Courtney, Kurt and subsequently Nirvana. Kurt appeared to have turned into everything he'd once despised. He was making radio-friendly rock, he was behaving like a superstar, and he was strung out on smack, the ultimate in wasted rock 'n' roll delirium. He spent a great deal of time protecting his wife and child, struggling to preserve his integrity and battling with addiction, his stomach pains, his and Courtney's media obsession, and the paranoia which ensued after his friends began pulling away from his junkie way of life.

Earlier on in the year, while in Belfast, with Nirvana, Kurt had been rushed to hospital when his methadone pills ran out, sparking off all manner of overdose rumours. By the time the band played

Reading Festival, Kurt's health was a major topic of music industry conversation. Just to prove how aware of all this he was, Kurt was wheeled on to the stage of Reading in a wheelchair wearing a surgical gown. He wound up the set by encouraging the crowd to declare their love for Courtney who was back in LA with the newly born Bean.

In September, Kurt and Courtney had a scuffle with Axl Rose of Guns 'n' Roses at the MTV awards, and around the same time, Kurt began openly attacking Pearl Jam. He'd known two members from their days with Green River, one of the original Sub Pop bands, and now believed they'd turned into little more than a semi alternative cock rock band. His bitterness and unease with his current superstar status was all too obvious, and although he finally made it up with Pearl Jam vocalist, Eddie Vedder, his view of the band was always tenuous, being intrinsically bound up with his suspicion of success.

To make matters worse for the inner workings of Nirvana, two British so called journalists (one of whom was a fanzine writer, the other a former boutique owner who went out with Shane MacGowan of The Pogues) attempted to write a Nirvana biography. It didn't take long for the band to realise that these women, Victoria Clarke and Britt Collins were simply looking for tabloid style muck, and so

they urged all their friends and acquaintances not to have any contact with them. Allegedly one of the women had managed to worm her way into the affections of Seattle lensman Charles Peterson, and was using him to help her with contacts, so by the time Nirvana sent out the warning signs, several interviews had already been conducted. Luckily though, Nirvana managed to put a legal stop on the book's publication, and commissioned Rolling Stone writer, Michael Azzerrad to write the official, although deliberately unauthorised, story.

After struggling through 1992, ravaged by problems both personal and professional, Nirvana entered 1993 with plans to record their third album, thereby quelling all rumours of their demise. They'd decided on former Big Black member Steve Albini (now of Shellac, and responsible for producing PJ Harvey's *'Rid Of Me'* album, as well as a zillion underground records) for producer, and went into the studio in February. Trouble was soon to follow though. A couple of months later, Albini announced that Geffen were unhappy with the mixes of the album, and had ordered them to be re-done. Other sources were whispering that Courtney was urging Kurt into re-mixing because the songs sounded too commercial. Eventually Kurt wrote a letter to Newsweek explaining that the band were re-mixing because they wanted to.

"Being commercial or anti-commercial is not what makes a good rock record." he wrote, *"It's the songs. And until we have the songs recorded the way we want them, Nirvana will not release this record."*

In June, *'In Utero'* (which was nearly titled *'I Hate Myself And I Want To Die'*) was completed, featuring two re-mixes by Scott Litt, the first singles to be taken from the album, *'Heart Shaped Box'* and *'All Apologies'*. Among the cover shots was a picture taken by top rock photographer Michael Lavine. During

'In Utero' was released on Geffen in September 1993 and would be the last studio album from Nirvana, including the ironic *'All Apologies'*.

Lavine's session, Kurt was so high he was nodding out throughout. Clearly his habit was back in full swing.

Kurt and Courtney hit the headlines again in July when they had a fight at their Seattle home. Neighbours called the police after a noisy argument broke out, supposedly about the presence of firearms in the house. Kurt wanted them, Courtney didn't, and the two ended up lashing out at each other. Seattle law stipulates that police action must always be taken in cases of domestic violence, so Kurt was carted off to jail, although Courtney later told the Seattle Times that her husband was not a violent man, and that she had been considerably upset by the episode. Later, a source close to the band revealed that the quarrel had in fact been about Kurt's drug habit.

'Heart Shaped Box' was released in August, and *'In Utero'* appeared in September. British rock

critics hailed the album as a personal masterpiece of Kurt's, whose lyrics delved into particularly emotional territory based largely on the previous year's troubles. Falling in love, becoming a father, coping with the intrusion of fame were all themes which popped up, meaning *'In Utero'* was neither the hardcore punk album Kurt had promised it would be, nor the commercial pop record certain factions of Nirvana's fanbase were hoping for. It was a startlingly good album, heavy with guitars and rich with melody, and above all, stood in defence of a human being's right to privacy.

Nirvana carried on throughout the rest of 1993, playing shows, doing interviews, and trying to live their lives. They brought in a second guitarist, 'Big' John Duncan of Goodbye Mr Mackenzie, to beef up the live sound, and replaced him with Pat Smear, previously of The Germs when Duncan returned to his own band. Life seemed better, but not for long.

A major European tour was lined up for the following spring to promote *'In Utero'*, and although everything started off well, crisis struck in Rome on March 4th when Kurt collapsed into a coma at his hotel. Courtney found him with blood coming out of his nose, and rushed him to hospital where 50 Rohypnol tablets were found in his stomach, Rohypnol, similar to Valium in its tranquillising effect, had been prescribed to Courtney, or so she claimed.

The incident took a decidedly sinister turn however, when a note from Kurt was found back in his hotel room, and although Nirvana's management denied it was suicide-related, with hindsight things were about to look very different.

Nirvana cancelled the rest of their tour and after three days in Rome's American Hospital, Kurt returned home to Seattle with Courtney. A month later, he once again attempted suicide. This time he succeeded. On April 8th, just before 9am, Kurt Cobain's body was found in a greenhouse above the garage of his home by an electrician who was installing a security system in the house. By this time Kurt had been missing for six days. The police were looking for him, Courtney had hired private investigators, but no one had tracked him down. When they did, it was too late.

Soon after the Rome incident it became apparent that Kurt was truly on a downward spiral. His relationship with Nirvana was in jeopardy, his relationship with Courtney wasn't exactly stable, he was feeling more and more guilty about playing music he no longer cared about, and coupled with his stomach pains and the peculiar state of mind which accompanies drug addiction, he was ready to quit life on earth. His heroin habit was destroying him and together with his friends, Courtney was taking serious measures to help him.

At one point she even threatened to leave him. The suicide attempt in Rome wasn't the only time Kurt threatened to leave for good. On March 18th Courtney called the police to the couple's Seattle home after Kurt locked himself inside a room with a gun, declaring that he intended to shoot himself. A year earlier he had overdosed on heroin and had to be revived by his wife, who administered a combination of certain drugs which brought him round, and in July of 1993, Courtney found Kurt unconscious in a hotel bathroom in New York, again after overdosing. Somehow Kurt managed to play with Nirvana that night. At the time nobody suspected a thing.

Towards the end of March 1994, Courtney flew to Los Angeles to detox from tranquillisers, hoping that Kurt would follow her. He didn't. Instead he got himself a gun with the help of Dylan Carlson from the Sub Pop band Earth. Once he'd taken the gun home Kurt travelled down to the Exodus Recovery Centre in the Daniel Freeman Marina Hospital in California's Marina del Rey. He stayed for two days, during which time he called Courtney for the last time, to tell her she'd made a great record (her second album, *'Live Through This'* was due out in a fortnight) and that he loved her. Shortly afterwards he escaped from the clinic, went back up to Seattle, wandered around for a few days, and finally barricaded himself inside his greenhouse, took a hit

of Valium and heroin, wrote a long note to Courtney and his fans, put a gun to his head, and pulled the trigger. He was identifiable only by his fingerprints.

A memorial service was held for him at the Seattle Unity Church on April 10th. Dave and Chris attended and Courtney was supported by her old friend, Kat Bjelland. Kurt's body was still with the medical examiners, but he was later cremated. On the same day a huge candlelight vigil was held in a park near Seattle's Space Needle. 5,000 fans were present.

The loss of Kurt Cobain has been sorely felt throughout the music industry and amongst his fans. His death seemed needless in so many ways. It left people feeling angry at him, at the insensitive workings of the music business and the media, at heroin, at the whole rocket experience of Nirvana. Yet even old photographs of the band's early days, when they were just three carefree bums from a tiny nowhere town, with nothing more complicated than making music on their minds, belie the roots of Kurt's outcome. He was always more complex than people realised, always walking the thin line. Eventually he became so caught up in emotional, physical and spiritual pain that he couldn't see a way out in this life, so he chose to end it. Maybe there's a lesson in all this, maybe just the sad tale of a lost boy with no hope left. At least he ensured his memory wouldn't die.

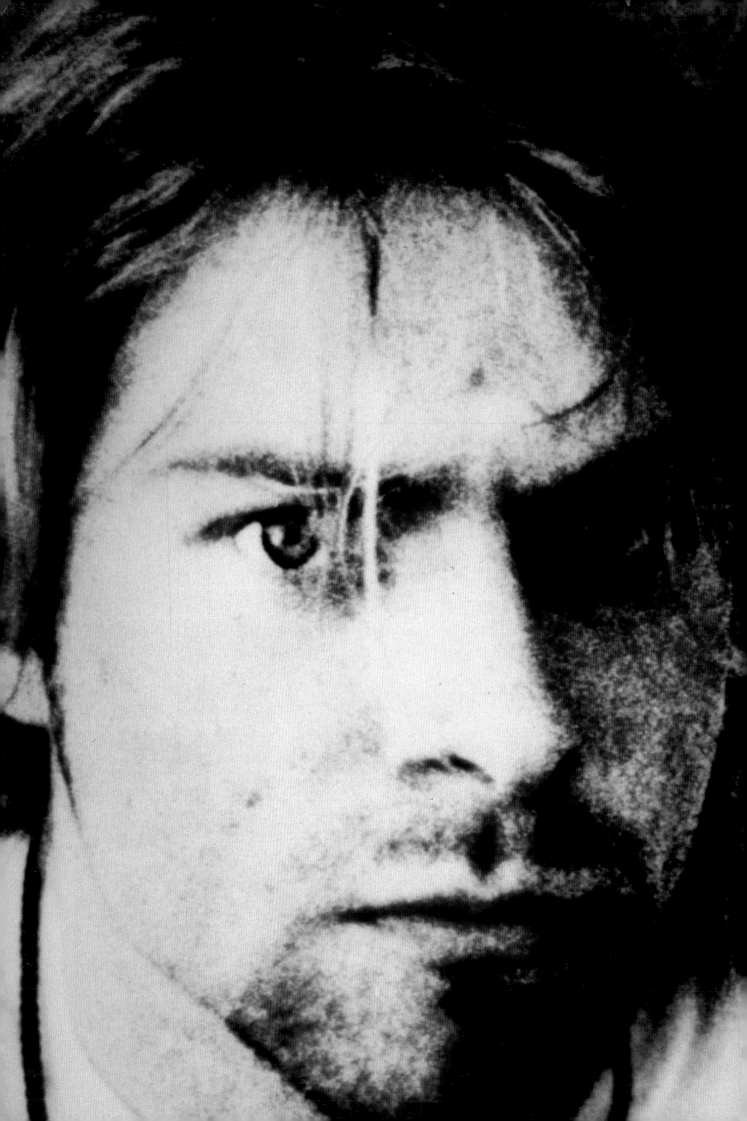

AFTERWORD

Since the tragedy of Kurt Cobain's suicide, Chris - now known as Krist Novoselic has become something of a political spokesperson for the environment and the plight of his people in Croatia. Dave Grohl has founded the Foo Fighters, who released their debut to much critical acclaim in mid-1995. And Courtney Love-Cobain continues to attract trouble, praise and intrigue with her inimitable behaviour and her band, Hole.

Life after Kurt goes on - but not without the legacy of his influence.

DISCOGRAPHY

SINGLES

LOVE BUZZ/BIG CHEESE
US Release Only
Sub Pop SP 23.
November 1988.

**BLEW/LOVE BUZZ/
BEEN A SON/STAIN**
UK Release
Tupelo TUP EP8/CDB.
December 1989.

SLIVER/DIVE
US Release Only
Sub Pop SP 72.
September 1990.

**MOLLY'S LIPS/
CANDY (by Fluid)**
US Release Only
Sub Pop SP 97. 1991

SLIVER/DIVE
UK Release
Tupelo TUP 25/EP25/CD 25.
January 1991.

**SMELLS LIKE TEEN
SPIRIT/DRAIN YOU**
Geffen DGC 5/DGCC 5/
DGCTP 5/ DGCT 5/DGCCD 5.
November 1991.

**COME AS YOU
ARE/ENDLESS, NAMELESS**
Geffen
DGC 7/DGCC 7/DGCTP 7/
DGCT 7/DGCTD 7.
March 11992.

LITHIUM/CURMUDGEON
Geffen DGCS 9/DGCSC
9/DGCTP 9/ DGCSD
9. July 1992.

IN BLOOM/POLLY (Live)
Geffen GFS 34/ GFSC 34/
GFSTP 34/ GFSTD 34.
November 1992.

**OH, THE GUILT/
PUSS (by the Jesus Lizard)**
Touch & Go TG83/ TG83CD.
February 1993.

**HEART SHAPED BOX/
MARIGOLD**
Geffen GFS 54/ GFSC 54/
GFST 54/ GFSTD 54.
August 1993.

**ALL APOLOGIES/
RAPE ME**
Geffen GFS 66/ GFCS 66/
GFSTD 66.
December 1993.

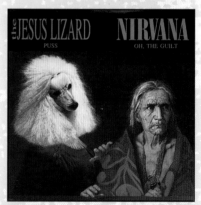

ALBUMS

BLEACH
US Release Only
Sub Pop SP 34.
June 1989.
Tracks:
Blew, Floyd the Barber, About a Girl, School, Love Buzz, Paper Cuts, Negative Creep, Scoff, Swap Meet, Mr. Moustache, Sifting, Big Cheese

BLEACH
Tupelo TUP LP 6/ TUP MC 6/ TUP CD 6.
August 1989.
Reissued in April 1992 (Geffen GEF 24433/ GEFC 24433/ GEFD 24433).

NEVERMIND
Geffen DGC 24425/ DGCC 24425 / DGCCD 24425/ DGCX 24425.
September 1991.
Tracks:
Smells Like Teen Spirit, In Bloom, Come As You Are, Breed, Lithium, Polly, Territorial Pissings, Drain You, Lounge Act, Stay Away, On A Plain, Something In The Way

HORMOANING
Australian and Japanese Release Only
Geffen
GEF 21711 / GED 21711.
1991.
Tracks:
Turnaround, Aneurysm, D-7, Son Of A Gun, Even In His Youth, Molly's Lips

INCESTICIDE
Geffen GEF 24504/ GEC 24504/ GED 24504.
December 1992.
Tracks:
Dive, Sliver, Stain, Been A Son, Turnaround, Molly's Lips, Son Of A Gun, (New Wave) Polly, Beeswax, Downer, Mexican Seafood, Hairspray Queen, Aero Zeppelin, Big Long Now, Aneurysm

IN UTERO
Geffen GEF 24536/ GEC 24536/ GED 24536.
September 1993.
Tracks:
Serve The Servants, Scentless Apprentice, Heart-Shaped Box, Rape Me, Frances Farmer Will Have Her Revenge On Seattle, Dumb, Very Ape, Milk It, Pennyroyal Tea, Radio Friendly Unit Shifter, tourette's, All Apologies, Gallons Of Rubbing Alcohol Flow Through The Strip

UNPLUGGED IN NEW YORK
Geffen GEF 24727/ GEC 24727/ GED 24727.
October 1994.
Tracks:
About A Girl, Come As You Are, Jesus Doesn't Want Me For A Sunbeam, The Man Who Sold The World, Pennyroyal Tea, Dumb, Polly, On A Plain, Something In The Way, Plateau, Oh Me, Lake Of Fire, All Apologies, Where Did You Sleep Last Night